The Path to Prosperity: Habits for a Fulfilling Life in Family, Finance, and Love

Arthur Anderson

The Path to Prosperity: Habits for a Fulfilling Life in Family, Finance, and Love

Arthur Anderson

Published by Arthur Anderson, 2024.

While every precaution has been taken in the preparation of this book, the publisher assumes no responsibility for errors or omissions, or for damages resulting from the use of the information contained herein.

THE PATH TO PROSPERITY: HABITS FOR A FULFILLING LIFE IN FAMILY, FINANCE, AND LOVE

First edition. March 17, 2024.

ISBN: 979-8224744411

Written by Arthur Anderson.

CONTENTS

Family Reading and Learning Habits: How to foster continuous education.

Entrepreneurship in the Family: Considerations for starting a successful family business.

The Importance of Family Traditions: How Traditions Can Strengthen Family Bonds.

Financial Communication Habits in Couples: Maintaining healthy financial conversations in a romantic relationship.

Family Goal Planning: Setting and pursuing goals together.

Building a Family Legacy: Considerations on Heritage and Inheritance.

Positive Parenting Habits: How to raise happy and healthy children.

Appreciation of the Little Things in Life: Focus on everyday happiness.

Celebration of Family Success: How to celebrate achievements and strengthen family bonds.

The Importance of Habits: Introduction to how habits can transform life in these three key areas.

In the vast journey of life, we often find ourselves searching for the path to prosperity. But what is prosperity, really? It's not simply the accumulation of material wealth, nor is it limited to achieving success in just one area of our lives. True prosperity is a balance, a harmony, an intersection of three essential elements: family, finances, and love. In "The Path to Prosperity: Habits for a Fulfilling Life in Family, Finance, and Love," we will explore how habits can be the compass guiding us toward this desired balance.

In our day-to-day lives, we operate on autopilot more than we realize. We perform routine tasks and make decisions without giving them much thought. These are our habits, the actions we repeat almost unconsciously. But what if we start paying attention to these habits? Could we consciously change those that hinder our prosperity and develop new ones that lead us to success in family, finances, and love?

This book is a journey of self-discovery and personal transformation. We will explore how every small daily act, every habit we cultivate, has the power to alter our reality in surprising ways. Habits not only shape our behavior but also forge our identity and determine our destiny.

In the pages ahead, we will discover how habits can be a driving force that enables us to improve communication in the family, cultivate empathy in our relationships, make wiser financial decisions, and nurture stronger loving connections. Through concrete examples and practical advice, we will learn how small changes in our daily routine can have a profound and lasting impact on our lives.

As we explore the key areas of family, finances, and love, we will discover that prosperity is not a distant goal but a path unfolding before us as we progress. Every habit we adopt will bring us one step closer to a fulfilling and satisfying life in these three fundamental areas.

So, prepare to embark on this exciting journey. Throughout these pages, you will find the inspiration and tools to become the architect of your own prosperity. Every word you read will remind you that you have the power to transform your life through the habits you choose to cultivate. Let's begin this extraordinary journey toward prosperity together!

Effective Communication in the Family: Tips for improving communication among family members.

Communication is the glue that binds a family together. It is the avenue through which we share our joys, concerns, achievements, and challenges. Yet, despite its critical importance, we often underestimate the impact that poor communication can have on our family relationships.

In "The Path to Prosperity," we recognize that effective communication is one of the strongest foundations for building a united and harmonious family. Improving how we communicate with our loved ones will not only strengthen family bonds but also open the door to deeper understanding and constructive conflict resolution.

Active Listening: True communication is not just speaking but also listening. Pay attention to what others are saying, show genuine interest, and ask questions to better understand their perspectives.

Quality Time: Dedicate quality time to being together as a family, without electronic distractions. This will foster meaningful conversations and strengthen bonds.

Expression of Feelings: Encourage family members to express their feelings openly and honestly. Create an environment where everyone feels safe sharing their emotions.

Nonverbal Communication: Remember that nonverbal communication is also powerful. Body language, eye contact, and facial expressions convey a lot. Ensure that your nonverbal cues reinforce your words.

Mutual Respect: Foster respect in all family conversations, even when discussing difficult topics. Avoid sarcasm, destructive criticism, and contempt.

Assertive Communication: Teach family members to express their needs and desires assertively, avoiding aggression or passivity. This will promote more effective conflict resolution.

Problem-Solving: Focus conversations on finding solutions to problems rather than blaming or pointing fingers. Work together towards solutions that benefit everyone.

Empathy: Practice empathy by trying to understand others' perspectives, even if you disagree. This will promote understanding and tolerance.

Regular Communication: Make regular communication a priority in the family. This means not only talking when problems arise but also celebrating achievements and happy moments.

Learning from Mistakes: Sometimes, communications fail. The important thing is to learn from mistakes and commit to improving communication in the future.

Empathy Habits in Family Relationships: How to cultivate empathy at home.

Empathy is the ability to understand and share the feelings of others. It is a fundamental skill in any relationship, but its importance becomes even more relevant in the family environment. Cultivating empathy at home not only strengthens family bonds but also creates an atmosphere where all members feel valued and understood.

In "The Path to Prosperity," we recognize that empathy is an essential pillar for building strong and healthy family relationships. Here, we will explore how developing empathy habits at home can positively transform family dynamics:

Behavior Modeling: As parents and caregivers, it is crucial to model empathy. Children learn by observing the adults around them, so showing empathy in your own interactions will teach them its importance.

Encourage Active Listening: Teach family members to actively listen to each other. This means not only hearing the words but also paying attention to the emotions behind them.

Promote Open Dialogue: Create an environment where everyone feels comfortable sharing their thoughts and feelings without fear of judgment or criticism.

Put Yourself in Others' Shoes: Encourage the practice of putting oneself in others' shoes. Encourage your children to think about how they would feel if they were in their sibling's or any other family member's situation.

Validate Emotions: Learn to validate the emotions of your loved ones, even if you don't fully understand them. Sometimes, knowing that someone understands and accepts your feelings is enough to relieve tension.

Show Empathy in Tough Times: In times of conflict or stress, empathy is needed most. Help family members see things from each other's perspective and seek solutions together.

Promote Open Communication: Encourage your children to communicate openly and honestly about their concerns and challenges. Empathy naturally arises when we understand others' struggles and joys.

Celebrate Differences: Recognize and celebrate differences within the family. Each member is unique, with their own thoughts, feelings, and perspectives. Learn to appreciate these differences and see them as a source of enrichment.

Practice Patience: Empathy often requires patience. Not everyone processes their emotions in the same way or at the same pace. Allow yourself and others the time needed to express their feelings.

Reinforce Empathy with Actions: Empathy is not just about words; it also involves actions. Help family members develop empathy by acting in ways that reflect understanding and support.

Family Financial Planning: Strategies for effectively managing finances as a family.

Financial planning is a crucial aspect of family life, and its importance should not be underestimated. When finances are effectively managed at home, it creates a solid foundation for economic well-being, security, and the ability to achieve short and long-term financial goals. In "The Path to Prosperity," we will explore how family financial planning can be a fundamental pillar for achieving prosperity in all areas of life.

Setting Joint Financial Goals: Initiating family financial planning involves all family members participating in identifying common financial goals. This could include short-term goals like a family vacation, as well as long-term goals like children's college education or retirement.

Creating a Family Budget: Budgeting is an essential tool for managing family income and expenses. It helps allocate resources efficiently and control unnecessary spending. Additionally, it allows the family to stay on track towards achieving their financial goals.

Promoting Financial Education: Investing time in educating all family members about basic financial concepts is crucial. This includes teaching children about the value of money, saving, and financial responsibility.

Establishing an Emergency Fund: An emergency fund is essential for dealing with unexpected expenses, such as home repairs or unforeseen medical expenses. By having a financial cushion, the family can avoid resorting to costly debts in difficult times.

Reducing Debt: Debt management is an important part of financial planning. The family should work to reduce credit card debts and loans with high-interest rates, freeing up resources for other financial goals.

Saving and Investing Wisely: Encourage regular saving and wise investment. Explore investment options that align with the family's financial goals and provide long-term growth opportunities.

Insurance and Estate Planning: Ensuring that the family has adequate insurance to protect against unforeseen events is essential. Additionally, estate planning can ensure that assets and inheritance are distributed according to the family's wishes in the future.

Regular Review and Adjustment: A family's financial situation can change over time. Therefore, it is essential to regularly review and adjust the financial plan to adapt to new circumstances and changing goals.

Involving Children: Involving children in family financial management from a young age can be a valuable educational experience. Teaching them to save, budget, and understand the value of money will provide them with lifelong financial skills.

Open Communication about Money: Communication about financial matters in the family should be open and transparent. All members should feel comfortable discussing money and contributing ideas and solutions.

Investment and Saving: Habits for building wealth and financial security.

Investment and saving are two fundamental pillars for building wealth and long-term financial security. In "The Path to Prosperity," we will explore how developing solid habits in these areas can make a significant difference in a family's ability to achieve financial goals and ensure a solid and prosperous future.

Here are some key strategies for building wealth and financial security through saving and investing:

Set Clear Goals: Before starting to save and invest, it is essential to have clear financial goals. Are you saving for your children's college education, for retirement, or to buy a home? Setting specific goals will give you direction and motivation.

Create a Savings Plan: Develop a savings plan that includes a budget reflecting your financial goals. Identify areas where you can cut expenses and allocate those funds to saving and investing.

Diversify Investments: Diversification is key to minimizing risk in investments. Don't put all your assets into a single investment. Instead, consider a diversified portfolio that includes stocks, bonds, real estate, and other investment vehicles.

Automatic Savings: Set up automatic transfers from your checking account to a savings or investment account. This will help you maintain savings discipline and ensure that funds are regularly allocated to your financial goals.

Control Unnecessary Expenses: Review your expenses and look for areas where you can cut back without sacrificing your quality of life. Small cuts in everyday expenses can add up to significant savings over time.

Continuous Financial Education: Stay informed about investment options and financial strategies. Financial education is an investment in itself and will help you make more informed decisions.

Long-Term Investments: Invest with a long-term horizon in mind. Markets can be volatile in the short term, but over time, investments tend to grow and provide more solid returns.

Save for Retirement: Contribute regularly to retirement accounts such as a 401(k) plan or an IRA to ensure financial security in retirement. Take advantage of employer contributions if possible.

Emergency Fund: Maintain a well-funded emergency fund in a liquid account to deal with unexpected expenses without resorting to debt.

Regular Reassessment: Regularly review your investments and financial goals. As your personal and economic circumstances change, adjust your financial plan accordingly.

Family Budget: How to establish and maintain an effective family budget.

The family budget is a vital tool in managing a family's finances. It's like a map that guides the use of income, ensuring that resources are allocated intelligently to meet needs, achieve financial goals, and maintain economic stability. In "The Path to Prosperity," we will explore the importance of establishing and maintaining an effective family budget, as well as practical strategies to achieve it.

Gather Financial Information: Start by collecting all relevant financial information. This includes your income, regular expenses (such as mortgage or rent, utilities, groceries, and insurance), debts, and any other financial obligations.

Set Financial Goals: Before creating a budget, define your short and long-term financial goals. These may include saving for a family vacation, paying off debts, creating an emergency fund, or retiring comfortably.

Record Income: Record all regular income your family receives, such as salaries, bonuses, rental income, or other sources.

List Expenses: List all monthly expenses, such as housing, utilities, food, transportation, insurance, entertainment, and other recurring expenses. Divide expenses into categories for easier organization.

Identify Variable Expenses: In addition to regular expenses, there are variable expenses, such as entertainment, dining out, and discretionary purchases. Record these expenses as well, as they are often a source of unnecessary spending.

Calculate Total Income and Expenses: sum up all income and expenses to get a complete picture of your current financial situation.

Adjust and Prioritize: If your expenses exceed your income, it's time to make adjustments. Prioritize your essential needs and financial goals over non-essential expenses.

Create a Monthly Budget: Use a spreadsheet or budgeting app to create a detailed monthly budget. Make sure to allocate funds for each expense category and for your financial goals.

Review and Update: The budget is not static; it should be reviewed and updated regularly. This will allow you to adapt to changes in income, unexpected expenses, or new financial goals.

Stick to the Budget: Once you've established a budget, stick to it. This will require discipline and control of spending, but it will help you keep your finances in order.

Save and Pay off Debts: Allocate part of your income to savings and debt reduction. This will help you build wealth and avoid accumulating costly debts.

Cultivate Open Communication: Transparency and open communication with other family members are critical to budget success. Everyone should be aware of financial goals and committed to following them.

The Psychology of Money: Exploration of the attitudes and beliefs surrounding money.

Money is a powerful force in our lives, not only for its ability to buy goods and services but also for the influence it has on our emotions, relationships, and sense of security. Our attitudes and beliefs about money, often rooted in personal and cultural experiences, can profoundly impact our ability to manage it effectively and achieve financial prosperity.

In "The Path to Prosperity," we go beyond the numbers and explore the psychology of money. Here, we examine some common attitudes and beliefs surrounding money and how they can affect our lives:

Beliefs about Self-Worth: Many people associate their self-worth with the amount of money they have. If you believe that you are valuable only when you have a large amount of money, you may experience stress and low self-esteem when facing financial difficulties.

Fear of Scarcity: The fear of not having enough money to cover basic needs or face emergencies can lead to constant anxiety. This fear of scarcity often leads to over-worrying about finances and the inability to enjoy the present.

Guilt and Shame: People often feel guilty or ashamed of their past financial decisions, especially if they have accumulated debts or experienced economic hardships. These feelings can interfere with the ability to make healthy financial decisions.

Comparison with Others: The tendency to compare oneself with others in terms of material wealth can lead to envy, resentment, and dissatisfaction. It is important to remember that financial situations vary widely, and not everyone has the same opportunities or challenges.

Avoidance of Financial Conversations: Many people avoid talking about money, whether out of shame, fear of conflict, or lack of knowledge. Lack of communication can lead to financial misunderstandings and relationship problems.

Short-Term Perspective: Focusing on instant gratification instead of long-term planning can lead to impulsive financial decisions and lack of preparation for the future.

Fear of Financial Failure: Fear of financial failure can lead to risk aversion and a lack of initiative to seek investment or entrepreneurial opportunities.

Limiting Beliefs: Believing that the financial situation cannot be changed or that one does not deserve prosperity can be a significant obstacle to improving financial management.

Money as a Source of Happiness: The belief that more money automatically leads to greater happiness can be misleading. There is always a desire for more, and happiness never seems lasting.

Spending Expectations: Setting unrealistic spending expectations, such as maintaining an extremely high standard of living, can lead to debt accumulation and lack of savings.

Financial Education for Children: Teaching children about money and financial responsibility.

Financial education is a crucial life skill that can make a significant difference in children's financial future. In "The Path to Prosperity," we recognize the importance of teaching children about money and financial responsibility from a young age. Here, we will explore how we can prepare the next generation with the skills and knowledge needed to make smart and responsible financial decisions.

The Importance of Financial Education for Children:

Laying the Foundation: Early financial education lays the foundation for a healthy relationship with money in adulthood. Children who understand basic financial concepts are more likely to make informed financial decisions and avoid debt problems in the future.

Decision-Making Skills: Teaching children to make financial decisions, such as saving, investing, and responsible spending, fosters critical decision-making skills that are applicable in all areas of life.

Avoiding Financial Problems: Financial education helps children understand financial risks and how to avoid problems such as excessive borrowing or scams.

Fostering Independence: As children gain financial knowledge, they become more independent in managing their money, giving them a sense of control and responsibility.

Preparing for the Future: Financial concepts, such as saving for higher education and retirement, should be introduced from a young age so that children understand the importance of planning their financial future.

Strategies for Teaching Financial Education to Children:

Open Communication: Talk to your children about money in an open and honest manner. Answer their questions and foster an environment where they can discuss financial topics without fear of judgment.

Task Allocation: Assign household chores or additional responsibilities to your children in exchange for an allowance or reward. This will teach them about the value of work and financial reward.

Family Budget: Include children in creating and reviewing the family budget. This will help them understand how income and expenses are managed in the home.

Saving and Responsible Spending: Teach them to save part of their allowance or gifted money and how to set saving goals. Also, explain the importance of responsible spending and how to avoid impulsive spending.

Price Comparison: Teach children to compare prices and look for deals when shopping. This will help them develop skills for making informed decisions when purchasing.

Basic Investment Concepts: As children grow, introduce them to basic investment concepts. They can start with savings accounts and move on to long-term investments as they gain experience.

Charity and Donations: Encourage charity and donation by teaching your children about the importance of helping others and making charitable contributions.

Personal Example: Be a financial role model for your children. Your actions and attitudes toward money have a significant impact on their financial development.

Continuous Education: As children grow, provide more advanced information about financial topics, such as debt management, retirement planning, and investing in the stock market.

Hands-On Learning: Take advantage of practical teaching opportunities, such as taking children shopping and comparing prices, helping them open a savings or investment account, or involving them in family financial projects.

Habits for a Healthy Loving Life: How to maintain strong loving relationships.

A solid and healthy loving relationship is a fundamental pillar in the pursuit of prosperity in family life. In "The Path to Prosperity," we explore the importance of cultivating habits that strengthen and enrich loving relationships. These habits not only improve the quality of life for the couple but also have a positive impact on all aspects of family life.

The Importance of a Healthy Loving Relationship:

Emotional Well-being: A solid loving relationship significantly contributes to the emotional well-being of family members. It provides emotional support, security, and a sense of belonging.

Effective Communication: Healthy relationships are based on open and effective communication. The ability to express thoughts and feelings honestly and respectfully is fundamental.

Conflict Resolution: Healthy couples know how to address and resolve disagreements constructively. This prevents conflicts from accumulating and becoming sources of stress.

Personal Growth: Solid loving relationships foster personal growth. Each member of the couple has the opportunity to learn, evolve, and support individual and shared goals.

Habits to Maintain a Strong Loving Relationship:

Open Communication: Establishing open and honest communication is essential. Ensure that both parties feel heard and understood. Foster an environment where difficult issues can be discussed without fear of judgment.

Empathy: Practice empathy, i.e., the ability to understand and share the feelings of others. Putting yourself in your partner's shoes will strengthen the emotional connection.

Quality Time: Dedicate quality time together. This includes not only romantic dates but also everyday moments of connection and appreciation.

Mutual Support: Support each other's goals and dreams. When both partners support each other, a sense of collaboration and mutual growth is created.

Stress Management: Learn to manage stress healthily. Stress can negatively affect the relationship, so it is important to develop strategies to deal with it.

Healthy Independence: While it is important to spend time together, it is also essential to maintain healthy independence. Each member of the couple should have time for individual interests and friendships.

Affection and Touch: Physical intimacy, such as hugs and kisses, is crucial for maintaining emotional and physical connection in the relationship.

Future Planning: Discuss your long-term goals as a couple and plan together. This gives you a shared direction and a common purpose.

Continuous Learning: The relationship evolves over time, so keep learning about yourself and your partner. Adapting to changing needs and desires is key to maintaining a strong relationship.

Respect and Admiration: Respect and admire your partner. Recognize and value their qualities and achievements. Mutual respect is a cornerstone of healthy relationships.

Conflict Resolution in Love: Strategies for addressing and resolving disagreements in a relationship.

In all romantic relationships, disagreements and conflicts are inevitable. However, what distinguishes solid and healthy couples is their ability to address and resolve these challenges constructively. In "The Path to Prosperity," we examine the importance of developing effective conflict resolution skills in a relationship, as well as practical strategies for maintaining harmony and understanding in the relationship.

The Importance of Conflict Resolution in Love:

Communication Strengthening: Conflicts offer opportunities to improve communication in the relationship. We learn to express our thoughts and feelings more effectively.

Relationship Strengthening: Resolving conflicts constructively can strengthen the relationship, as it demonstrates both parties' commitment to working together to overcome obstacles.

Prevention of Resentment Accumulation: Conflict resolution prevents unresolved issues from accumulating and becoming sources of long-term resentment and tension.

Personal and Relationship Growth: Overcoming disagreements can lead to personal growth and a stronger relationship, as both parties learn to better understand each other and compromise.

Strategies for Conflict Resolution in a Relationship:

Open Communication: Open and honest communication is key. Both partners should feel comfortable expressing their thoughts and emotions without fear of judgment.

Active Listening: Actively listening to your partner is essential. Pay attention to what they say, show genuine interest, and validate their feelings.

Avoid Blame and Criticism: Avoid blaming or criticizing your partner during a discussion. Instead, use "I" statements to express how you feel and how the situation affects you.

Seek Solutions, Not Blame: Instead of focusing on who is to blame, focus together on finding solutions. Work as a team to address the problem.

Take a Break: If the discussion becomes intense, it's okay to take a break. Sometimes, a brief break can help cool tempers and return to the conversation with a calmer mind.

Compromise: Both parties should be willing to compromise and find solutions that satisfy both. The goal is the well-being of the relationship as a whole.

Learn from Conflicts: Each conflict can be a learning opportunity. Reflect on what triggered the conflict and how you can avoid similar problems in the future.

Maintain Respect: Even in the midst of an argument, maintain respect for your partner. Personal attacks and contempt should be avoided at all costs.

Seek Professional Help: If conflicts persist or become overwhelming, consider seeking the help of a therapist or couples counselor. Sometimes, a neutral third party can provide valuable perspectives.

Celebrate Resolution: Once you've reached a resolution, celebrate together. Acknowledge the effort you put into resolving the conflict and reinforce it with affection and appreciation.

Meditation and Mindfulness in Family Life: How mindfulness can enhance relationships.

In today's busy modern life, families often find themselves caught up in a hectic pace, which can lead to stress and tension in relationships. Meditation and mindfulness offer a respite from this hustle and can be powerful tools for improving family life quality. In "The Path to Prosperity," we explore how the practice of mindfulness can strengthen family bonds, foster empathy and effective communication, and promote harmony at home.

The Importance of Mindfulness in Family Life:

Stress Reduction: Meditation and mindfulness are effective in reducing stress in both adults and children. A less stressful environment at home promotes healthier relationships.

Emotional Connection: Mindfulness fosters greater emotional connection among family members. By being present and mindful of each other, the relationship is strengthened.

Improved Communication: Mindfulness teaches to listen more attentively and empathetically. This improves communication in the family, as each member feels valued and heard.

Promotion of Empathy: Practicing empathy is essential for healthy relationships. Mindfulness promotes empathy by encouraging understanding of others' perspectives and feelings.

Strategies for Introducing Mindfulness into Family Life:

Family Meditation Sessions: Regularly dedicate time to family meditation sessions. This can be as simple as sitting together in silence for a few minutes and focusing on breathing.

Gratitude Practices: Foster gratitude in daily life. Encourage family members to express what they are grateful for each day.

Mindful Walks: Take mindful walks as a family. Observe nature, sounds, and sensations around you without distractions.

Digital Detox: Establish device-free times in the family, where everyone disconnects and spends quality time together.

Conscious Breathing: Teach conscious breathing techniques that can be used to calm down in moments of tension.

Mindfulness Games: Incorporate games that promote mindfulness, such as board games that require concentration or family yoga exercises.

Open Dialogue: Encourage open conversations about the benefits of mindfulness in the family. Encourage everyone to share their experiences and discoveries.

Lead by Example: Be a mindfulness role model. Children often learn best by observing adults' behavior.

Practice Patience: Mindfulness teaches patience. Encourage family members to be more tolerant and patient with each other.

Celebrate Progress: Celebrate achievements in the practice of mindfulness in the family. Recognize and reward effort and positive changes in family relationships.

Gratitude and Appreciation Habits: Fostering gratitude in daily life.

Gratitude is a powerful force that can transform how we experience life. In "The Path to Prosperity," we recognize the importance of cultivating habits of gratitude and appreciation in daily life. These habits not only make us feel better but also have a positive impact on our relationships, mental health, and overall perception of life.

The Importance of Gratitude in Daily Life:

Enhances Emotional Well-being: Gratitude is linked to greater life satisfaction and a decrease in feelings of depression and anxiety. By focusing on what we have rather than what is lacking, we experience greater emotional well-being.

Strengthens Relationships: Expressing gratitude towards others strengthens interpersonal relationships. When we appreciate and acknowledge the people around us, we foster deeper and more meaningful connections.

Shifts Perspective: Gratitude changes how we view the world. Instead of taking what we have for granted, we begin to see the beauty in small things and find joy in the everyday.

Reduces Stress: Regular practice of gratitude is associated with stress reduction and increased ability to cope with difficult situations.

Habits to Foster Gratitude in Daily Life:

Gratitude Journal: Keeping a gratitude journal is an effective practice. Every day, write down three things you are grateful for. They can be simple things like a hot cup of coffee or more significant moments like support from a loved one.

Expressions of Thanks: Express your gratitude verbally or in writing to the people around you. Do not underestimate the power of a simple "thank you" or a note of appreciation.

Gratitude Meditation: Dedicate time in your meditation routine to focus on gratitude. Visualize the things you are grateful for and feel that gratitude in your heart.

Focus on the Positive: Practice shifting your focus to the positive in difficult situations. Instead of lamenting what went wrong, look for lessons or positive aspects.

Acts of Kindness: Regularly perform acts of kindness towards others. Helping others and doing good can generate feelings of gratitude and appreciation.

Nightly Reflection: Before going to bed, reflect on the things you are grateful for in the day. This can help you end the day on a positive note.

Teach Children: Foster gratitude in your children. Teach them to appreciate what they have and to express gratitude towards others.

Appreciation of Nature: Spend time outdoors and appreciate the beauty of nature. Connecting with nature can inspire feelings of gratitude.

Volunteering: Engage in volunteering activities. Helping those in need can increase your appreciation for what you have in your own life.

Share Gratitude Stories: Share gratitude stories within the family. Encourage. family members to share their own experiences of thankfulness.

Stress Management in the Family: Techniques to reduce family stress.

Family life can be rewarding and full of love, but it can also be stressful on many occasions due to daily demands and responsibilities. In "The Path to Prosperity," we recognize the importance of addressing and managing family stress effectively. By adopting techniques and strategies to reduce stress, we not only improve the quality of life for each family member but also strengthen family bonds and promote a healthier home environment.

The Importance of Reducing Stress in the Family:

Family Well-being: A less stressful family environment contributes to the overall well-being of all family members. When stress is reduced, a happier and healthier home is fostered.

Improved Communication: Stress can negatively affect communication within the family. By reducing stress, more effective communication and mutual understanding are facilitated.

Increased Resilience: When the family learns to manage stress effectively, it becomes more resilient to life's challenges and changes.

Relationship Strengthening: By addressing stress collaboratively, family bonds are strengthened. The family becomes a support system rather than an additional source of stress.

Techniques to Reduce Family Stress:

Open Communication: Foster an environment where all family members feel comfortable sharing their concerns and emotions. Open communication can help prevent unnecessary conflicts.

Task and Responsibility Allocation: Distribute tasks and responsibilities fairly within the family. This prevents one person from taking on an excessive workload and stress.

Establishment of Routines: Predictable routines provide structure and reduce stress. Set schedules for meals, schoolwork, and family time.

Quality Time: Dedicate quality time as a family. Set regular moments for fun and relaxing activities together.

Relaxation Practices: Introduce relaxation techniques such as meditation, deep breathing, or yoga into the family routine. These practices can help alleviate stress.

Family Exercise: Physical exercise is an excellent way to reduce stress. Engage in sports activities or take walks together as a family.

Digital Limits: Set boundaries for electronic device use. Excessive screen time can contribute to stress and family disconnection.

Resilience Building: Help family members develop coping skills and resilience. Teach them to manage stress effectively.

Mutual Support: Foster an environment of mutual support within the family. Each member should feel they can turn to others in times of need.

Leisure Time Planning: Schedule leisure time in the family agenda. Establishing moments to rest and enjoy together is essential for stress reduction.

Seek Professional Help: If family stress becomes overwhelming or persistent, consider seeking the help of a family therapist or counselor. They can provide guidance and additional strategies.

Family Time Planning: How to make the most of time together.

In modern life, where schedules are filled with commitments and activities, finding quality time to spend with family can be a challenge. However, family time planning is essential for strengthening bonds, creating meaningful memories, and promoting a sense of unity. In "The Path to Prosperity," we explore how making the most of time together can improve family life in all its dimensions.

The Importance of Family Time Planning:

Emotional Connection: Spending quality time together strengthens the emotional connection among family members. Face-to-face interaction promotes understanding and mutual affection.

Lasting Memories: Shared experiences create lasting memories that enrich family life. Children, in particular, value these experiences and carry them with them as they grow.

Improved Communication: Family time offers opportunities for improved communication. Relaxing and fun moments are ideal for discussing life's challenges and successes.

Tradition Strengthening: Family time planning allows for establishing and maintaining family traditions. These traditions create a sense of belonging and continuity across generations.

Strategies for Making the Most of Family Time:

Family Agenda: Establish a family agenda to coordinate activities and ensure there is time for family amid daily obligations.

Themed Nights: Schedule themed nights at home, such as movie nights, board game nights, or family cooking nights.

Outdoor Outings: Organize outdoor excursions, such as hikes, bike rides, or visits to local parks. Nature provides an ideal setting for family relaxation and play.

Family Lessons: Learn something new together as a family, whether it's learning to cook a new recipe, taking art classes, or learning to play a musical instrument.

Family Vacations: Plan family vacations to create special memories. Even short trips can be exciting and enriching.

Quality Time: When with family, focus on being present and fully engaged in activities. Set aside digital distractions and enjoy the moment.

Special Celebrations: Celebrate milestones and important events as a family, such as birthdays, anniversaries, and academic or professional achievements.

Volunteer Together: Engage in volunteer activities as a family. Helping others can be a rewarding experience for everyone.

Mutual Support: Foster an environment of mutual support within the family. Encourage everyone to share their interests and desires so that family time planning is inclusive.

Flexibility: While having plans is important, being flexible is also crucial. Sometimes, the most meaningful moments happen spontaneously.

Regular Family Meetings: Establish regular family meetings where everyone can express their thoughts, desires, and concerns about family time.

Physical Health and Family Well-being: Habits for a healthy family life.

Physical health and well-being are crucial for the overall well-being of the family. Maintaining healthy habits together not only improves quality of life but also promotes family unity and sets a valuable example for children. In "The Path to Prosperity," we explore how fostering habits of physical health and well-being in family life can have a positive impact on all key areas of prosperity.

The Importance of Physical Health and Family Well-being:

Increased Energy and Vitality: Adopting healthy habits promotes greater energy and vitality throughout the family. This allows family members to feel better physically and emotionally.

Stress Reduction: Regular exercise and a healthy diet are effective in reducing stress in the family. A less stressful home contributes to the well-being of everyone.

Family Bond Strengthening: Participating in physical and well-being activities together strengthens family bonds. Cooperation and mutual support are fostered when working towards common health goals.

Role Modeling: Parents who set an example of healthy living have a lasting impact on their children's habits. Children learn from the adults around them, so it's essential to be a role model.

Habits to Foster Physical Health and Well-being in the Family:

Family Exercise: Plan physical activities that the family can enjoy together, such as hikes, bike rides, swimming, or playing outdoor games.

Healthy Eating: Promote balanced nutrition within the family. Cook nutritious meals at home and teach children about healthy food choices.

Screen Limits: Set limits on screen time to encourage physical activity instead of time spent in front of electronic devices.

Outdoor Time: Dedicate regular time to being outdoors. Whether in the backyard, at a park, or in nature, the outdoors offers opportunities for exercise and relaxation.

Consistent Sleep Schedule: Establish regular sleep schedules for all family members. Adequate sleep is essential for physical and mental health.

Recreational Activities: Encourage recreational activities such as team sports, dancing, or yoga. These activities can be fun and healthy for everyone.

Stress Management: Teach family members stress management techniques such as meditation and deep breathing to help them cope with daily tensions.

Regular Medical Check-ups: Schedule regular medical check-ups for all family members. Early detection of health issues is key to long-term well-being.

Active Rest: Instead of watching TV or playing video games, promote active rest such as taking a post-dinner walk instead of sitting in front of the television.

Continuous Learning: Educate the family about the benefits of a healthy lifestyle. Encourage everyone to learn about nutrition, exercise, and well-being together.

Celebration of Achievements: Celebrate health achievements as a family. Recognize the efforts and achievements of each family member in pursuit of a healthy lifestyle.

Personal Development: Fostering personal growth in all family members.

Personal development is a continuous journey of self-discovery and growth that can greatly enrich the life of every family member. In "The Path to Prosperity," we recognize the importance of fostering personal development within the family as an essential component for achieving prosperity in all key areas of life.

The Importance of Personal Development in the Family:

Individual Growth: Fostering personal development in each family member promotes individual growth. Each person has the opportunity to discover their talents, passions, and potential.

Self-awareness: Personal development involves increased self-awareness. Family members can learn more about themselves, their values, and personal goals.

Improved Relationships: When individuals work on their personal development, they often become more empathetic, understanding, and capable of establishing healthier relationships.

Resilience: Personal development teaches resilience skills that are valuable in challenging times. Family members can face difficult situations when they have cultivated their personal growth.

Strategies to Foster Personal Development in the Family:

Open Communication: Foster open communication within the family. Encourage everyone to share their personal goals, achievements, and challenges.

Mutual Support: Provide mutual support in personal development efforts. Celebrate each family member's achievements and provide encouragement in challenging times.

Setting Personal Goals: Encourage each family member to set personal goals. This may include academic, professional, sports, or creative goals.

Continuous Education: Promote continuous education within the family. Encourage reading, exploration of new topics, and pursuit of learning opportunities.

Skills Development: Provide opportunities for skills development. This could include enrolling in classes, workshops, or extracurricular activities.

Family Mentoring: Establish a mentoring system within the family. Younger members can learn from the experiences and knowledge of adults.

Time for Reflection: Encourage time for personal reflection. This may include meditation, keeping a gratitude journal, or practicing mindfulness.

Exploration of Passions: Encourage each family member to explore their passions and interests. This can lead to exciting discoveries and personal growth.

Leading by Example: Parents and adults in the family can serve as role models by committing to their own personal development. Children often mimic what they see in adults.

Goal Evaluation: Periodically review personal goals as a family. This allows for adjustments and adaptations to goals based on changing needs and desires.

Celebration of Personal Successes: Celebrate each family member's personal successes and achievements. Recognize and value the effort and progress toward personal growth.

Family Reading and Learning Habits: How to foster continuous education.

Learning is a journey that never ends, and when fostered within the family, it can enrich the lives of all its members. In "The Path to Prosperity," we recognize the importance of cultivating reading and learning habits within the family as a means to promote intellectual growth, mutual understanding, and prosperity in all key areas of life.

The Importance of Reading and Learning Habits in the Family:

Cognitive Development: Reading and continuous learning stimulate the cognitive development of all family members. An active mind is a healthy mind.

Broadening Horizons: Through reading and learning, the family can explore new topics, cultures, and perspectives, enriching their understanding of the world.

Improved Communication: Sharing readings and discussing learning topics can improve communication within the family, promoting meaningful conversations and mutual understanding.

Empowerment: Knowledge is power. Fostering continuous education within the family empowers its members to make informed decisions in all areas of life.

Strategies to Foster Reading and Learning Habits in the Family:

Family Library: Create a family library with a variety of books suitable for all ages and interests. Encourage everyone to choose books and share their discoveries.

Reading Sessions: Dedicate time for reading sessions as a family. This may include reading stories to children or sharing books and articles of mutual interest.

Family Book Clubs: Organize a family book club. Choose a book to read together, then discuss it as a family.

Visits to Libraries and Museums: Plan visits to libraries, museums, and other learning venues as a family. These outings can be educational and fun.

Online Learning: Use online resources for learning. There are many educational platforms offering courses and content for all ages.

Study Support: Provide a quiet study space and support for children in their schoolwork. Encourage teenagers to take responsibility for their own learning.

Meaningful Conversations: Foster meaningful conversations about what has been learned. Encourage everyone to share their ideas and knowledge.

Setting Learning Goals: As a family, set learning goals for the year. This may include learning a new language, studying an artistic discipline, or exploring a historical era.

Documentaries and Educational Movies: Enjoy documentaries and educational movies as a family. Then, discuss and reflect on what has been learned.

Active Participation: Encourage active participation in education. Support extracurricular activities and self-directed learning by family members.

Celebration of Learning: Celebrate achievements and successes in the learning of each family member. Recognize and value the effort in the knowledge acquisition process.

Adult Leadership: Adults in the family can serve as role models by committing to their own continuous learning. Children often imitate what they see in adults.

Entrepreneurship in the Family: Considerations for starting a successful family business.

Starting a family business can be an exciting and challenging experience at the same time. In "The Path to Prosperity," we recognize the importance of exploring entrepreneurship within the family as a means to achieve prosperity in all key areas of life. Here, we will examine fundamental considerations for starting and maintaining a successful family business.

The Importance of Entrepreneurship in the Family:

Family Unity: Entrepreneurship in the family can strengthen family bonds by creating a shared goal and a sense of belonging to a common project.

Transmission of Values: A family business provides a unique opportunity to transmit values, knowledge, and skills from generation to generation.

Financial Independence: A successful business can provide financial independence to the family, contributing to overall financial prosperity.

Flexibility: Family entrepreneurship often allows for greater flexibility in terms of schedules and lifestyle, which can improve family quality of life.

Considerations for Successful Entrepreneurship in the Family:

Planning and Strategy: Before starting the business, develop a comprehensive business plan that includes goals, strategies, business structure, and realistic financial projections.

Clear Roles: Define clear roles and responsibilities for each family member involved in the business. This helps avoid conflicts and ensures smooth operation.

Open Communication: Foster open and honest communication in the family and in the business. Effective communication is key to solving problems and making informed decisions.

Separation of Personal and Professional: Establish clear boundaries between personal and professional life. Prevent family conflicts from affecting the business and vice versa.

Continuous Education: Invest in the education and professional development of family members involved in the business. Staying updated is essential for long-term success.

Business Ethics: Establish a business culture based on ethical values and solid principles. Strong business ethics are essential for reputation and customer trust.

Succession Plan: Consider a succession plan from the outset. Define how the business will be transferred to future generations and how transitions will be handled.

Constant Evaluation: Regularly evaluate business performance and adjust strategies as needed. Adaptability is key in the business environment.

External Support: Seek advice and external support when necessary. Consult business experts or a network of family entrepreneurs.

Celebration of Achievements: Celebrate successes and achievements in the family business. Recognize and value the effort and dedication of all family members involved.

Work-Life Balance: Maintain a healthy balance between work and personal life. Prevent the business from completely absorbing family life.

The Importance of Family Traditions: How Traditions Can Strengthen Family Bonds.

Family traditions are fundamental pillars that bind generations together and strengthen family ties over time. In "The Path to Prosperity," we recognize the profound importance of family traditions and how they can contribute to prosperity in all key areas of life. Here, we will explore why these traditions are so vital and how they can enrich family life.

The Significant Importance of Family Traditions:

Cultural Heritage: Family traditions often reflect the cultural heritage and roots of the family. Maintaining these traditions is a way of honoring and preserving cultural identity.

Coherence and Continuity: Traditions provide coherence and continuity to family life. They offer a structure that endures across generations, even in times of change.

Family Unity: Traditions foster family unity by providing meaningful moments to connect and create shared memories.

Values and Virtues: Many traditions convey important values and virtues, such as gratitude, generosity, solidarity, and mutual understanding.

How to Strengthen Family Bonds Through Traditions:

Identification of Traditions: Identify and acknowledge existing family traditions. These may include birthday celebrations, religious festivities, special meals, annual trips, or other recurring activities.

Creation of Traditions: Create new family traditions. These can be as simple as a monthly movie night or as significant as an annual family trip.

Involvement of Everyone: Encourage all family members to contribute to the creation and maintenance of traditions. Active participation promotes a sense of belonging and commitment.

Adaptability: Be flexible in adapting traditions as the family grows and changes. Traditions can evolve over time to meet changing needs and desires.

Storytelling: Share family stories and anecdotes related to traditions. This connects generations and strengthens the sense of family history.

Celebration of Achievements: Use traditions as opportunities to celebrate family accomplishments, such as graduations, weddings, anniversaries, and other significant milestones.

Active Participation: Foster active participation of children in traditions. These experiences can enrich their sense of identity and belonging.

Reflection and Gratitude: Promote reflection and gratitude during traditions. These moments can be opportunities to appreciate what they have and strengthen family bonds.

Recognition of Cultural Traditions: If your family has a specific cultural heritage, make sure to transmit and celebrate traditions related to it.

Documentation and Memories: Document family traditions and memories. This can be through photographs, scrapbooks, or family journals.

Special Family Gatherings: Organize special family gatherings where traditions can be celebrated and maintained. This can be especially valuable if the family is geographically dispersed.

Continued Commitment: Show continued commitment to family traditions. As generations grow, these traditions will be an important legacy they share with the future.

Financial Communication Habits in Couples: Maintaining healthy financial conversations in a romantic relationship.

Financial communication in a romantic relationship can be a delicate topic, but it's essential for building a solid foundation for the future. In "The Path to Prosperity," we recognize the importance of developing effective financial communication habits in couples as a means to achieve prosperity in all key areas of life. Below, we will explore why this skill is crucial and how healthy financial conversations can be cultivated in a relationship.

The Importance of Financial Communication in a Couple:

Transparency: Financial communication promotes transparency and trust in the relationship. When both partners are informed about finances, they feel more secure and connected.

Joint Planning: It allows for joint planning of short and long-term financial goals. This helps ensure that both are on the same page regarding their shared financial objectives.

Conflict Resolution: Open communication about money facilitates the resolution of financial conflicts before they escalate into larger issues.

Shared Responsibility: When both partners participate in financial decision-making, responsibility is shared, relieving pressure on a single individual.

How to Maintain Healthy Financial Conversations in a Romantic Relationship:

Establish a Safe Space: Create an environment of trust and respect where both feel comfortable discussing money without fear of judgment or criticism.

Schedule Talking Times: Set regular times to discuss finances, such as once a month or before making major financial decisions.

Active Listening: Practice active listening by genuinely paying attention to what your partner has to say. Avoid interrupting and show empathy towards their concerns and opinions.

Shared Financial Goals: Identify and set shared financial goals. These may include saving for a trip, buying a home, or retirement.

Joint Budgeting: Work together to create a family budget. This will help you track expenses and allocate funds efficiently to reach your goals.

Discuss Financial Values: Share your financial values and listen to your partner's. This can help understand each other's priorities and preferences.

Emergency Planning: Discuss how you would handle unexpected financial situations together, such as job loss or medical expenses.

Expense Division: Determine how you will divide expenses in the relationship. Some couples choose to contribute in proportion to their incomes, while others may prefer a more equitable approach.

Avoid Blame or Criticism: Avoid blaming or criticizing your partner for past financial decisions. Instead, focus your efforts on solutions and how you can move forward together.

Joint Financial Education: If one partner has more financial knowledge, share that information in an understandable way and engage in financial education together.

Seek Professional Help: If you struggle to resolve financial issues, consider seeking the help of a financial advisor or couples counselor.

Celebration of Achievements: Celebrate financial milestones together, whether small or large. Recognize and value each other's efforts to reach your goals.

Family Goal Planning: Setting and pursuing goals together.

Family goal planning is a powerful process that can unite family members toward a common goal. In "The Path to Prosperity," we recognize the importance of setting and pursuing goals together as a means to achieve prosperity in all key areas of life. Below, we will explore why this practice is valuable and how family goals can be established and worked on effectively.

The Importance of Family Goal Planning:

Cooperation and Collaboration: Setting family goals fosters cooperation and collaboration among family members. Everyone works together towards a common objective.

Clarity of Purpose: Goal planning provides clarity of purpose and direction. It helps the family focus on what truly matters to them.

Motivation and Commitment: Family goals can be a source of motivation and commitment. When everyone is committed to a goal, they are more likely to strive to achieve it.

Bonds Strengthening: Pursuing goals together strengthens family bonds by creating shared memories and a sense of collective achievement.

How to Establish and Work on Family Goals Effectively:

Family Planning Meeting: Organize regular family meetings to discuss goals. This can be monthly or quarterly, depending on the complexity of the goals.

Involve Everyone: Ensure all family members have the opportunity to contribute to goal discussion and planning. Even children can have a role in selecting age-appropriate goals.

Define Clear Goals: Make sure goals are well-defined and specific. For example, instead of "travel more," set the goal of "taking a family trip to a new destination every year."

Goal Prioritization: If you have multiple goals, prioritize them. This will help the family focus on what's most important and avoid feeling overwhelmed.

Set Deadlines: Assign realistic deadlines for each goal. These deadlines provide a sense of urgency and help keep everyone accountable.

Develop an Action Plan: Create a detailed action plan outlining the steps needed to achieve each goal. This may include specific tasks for each family member.

Responsibility Division: Assign responsibilities according to each family member's skills and preferences. Everyone should have a role in executing the plan.

Tracking and Evaluation: Regularly track progress towards goals and assess whether adjustments to the plan are necessary.

Celebrate Achievements: Celebrate milestones and accomplishments along the way to goals. Recognize and appreciate the efforts and achievements of all family members.

Adaptability: Be flexible and willing to adjust goals if circumstances or family priorities change.

Teaching Values: Use goal planning as an opportunity to teach important values, such as perseverance, responsibility, and collaboration.

Review and Reflection: At the end of a designated period, review progress and reflect on what has been learned in the process of pursuing goals together.

Building a Family Legacy: Considerations on Heritage and Inheritance.

Building a family legacy transcends time and is an act of love and care towards future generations. In "The Path to Prosperity," we recognize the importance of considering heritage and inheritance as integral parts of prosperity in all key areas of life. Here, we will explore why building a family legacy is significant and how considerations related to heritage and inheritance can be addressed.

The Significant Importance of a Family Legacy:

Perpetuation of Values: A family legacy transmits values, beliefs, and traditions to future generations, keeping alive the principles that are important to the family.

Financial Security: Proper estate planning can provide financial security to the family, providing resources for future needs such as children's education or retirement.

Growth and Empowerment: A well-built legacy can empower future generations to achieve their goals and dreams. It can include financial resources, education, and opportunities.

Family Unity: Inheritance and heritage can unite the family around common goals and shared objectives, strengthening family bonds.

Important Considerations on Heritage and Inheritance:

Will and Estate Planning: Consult with an estate planning attorney to ensure your wishes are reflected in a valid will and succession plan.

Tax Planning: Understand the tax implications of your estate and seek strategies to minimize estate taxes legally.

Asset Distribution: Consider how you wish to distribute your assets and belongings to your heirs. Think about the impact this will have on the family and their well-being.

Financial Education: Invest in the financial education of your heirs. Teach them about money management, investing, and responsible financial management.

Charity and Philanthropy: Consider including charity and philanthropy in your estate planning. You can establish family foundations or donate to causes that are meaningful to you and your family.

Keep Records Updated: Make sure to keep updated records of your assets, debts, investments, and other financial aspects to facilitate the transition to your heirs.

Open Communication: Talk to your family about your wishes and expectations regarding heritage and inheritance. Open communication can prevent future conflicts.

Long-Term Planning: Think about how you want your legacy to endure over time. This may include wealth protection across generations and the promotion of family values.

Regular Review: Regularly review your estate plan to ensure it remains relevant and aligns with your changing goals and family circumstances.

Professional Advice: Seek the advice of financial and legal professionals to ensure your estate plan is sound and complies with current laws and regulations.

Clear Documentation: Ensure all legal documents related to your estate are in order and easily accessible to your heirs.

Celebration of Legacy: Celebrate and honor the family legacy. This may include family events, storytelling, and the promotion of family traditions.

Positive Parenting Habits: How to raise happy and healthy children.

Positive parenting is a fundamental aspect of family prosperity and ultimately contributes to prosperity in all key areas of life. In "The Path to Prosperity," we recognize the importance of cultivating habits that foster the well-being and development of children, which in turn strengthens family unity. Below, we explore why positive parenting is essential and how habits for raising happy and healthy children can be developed.

The Importance of Positive Parenting:

Healthy Development: Positive parenting provides a nurturing environment for the healthy physical, emotional, cognitive, and social development of children.

Self-Esteem and Confidence: It fosters self-esteem and confidence in children by providing them with support, love, and emotional security.

Effective Communication: It establishes a solid foundation for effective communication between parents and children, facilitating mutual understanding and conflict resolution.

Social Skills: It helps children develop positive social skills, such as empathy, respect, and problem-solving.

Resilience: It teaches children to face challenges and difficulties constructively, fostering emotional resilience.

Habits for Positive Parenting:

Love and Affection: Show love and affection to your children regularly. Affection and attention are essential for their emotional well-being.

Open Communication: Encourage open and honest communication. Actively listen to your children and respect their opinions and feelings.

Set Clear Boundaries: Establish clear boundaries and rules at home. Boundaries provide security and structure for children.

Model Positive Behavior: Be a positive role model. Children learn by observing adults' behavior.

Rewards and Consequences: Use appropriate rewards and consequences to shape behavior. Focus on positive reinforcement when children behave well.

Quality Time: Spend quality time with your children. Engage in activities that interest them and promote their development.

Encourage Autonomy: Encourage independence and age-appropriate decision-making. This helps children develop self-control and responsibility.

Positive Discipline: Opt for positive discipline instead of physical or emotional punishment. Positive discipline focuses on teaching and guiding rather than punishing.

Promote Conflict Resolution: Teach your children effective conflict resolution skills, such as speaking and listening, and seeking solutions together.

Support Education: Value education and support your children's learning. Be actively involved in their education and foster a love for learning.

Encourage Empathy: Teach your children to be empathetic and considerate towards others. Talk about the importance of understanding and respecting others' feelings.

Promote Health: Establish healthy habits in the family, such as a balanced diet, regular exercise, and sufficient rest.

Boost Self-Esteem: Help your children build positive self-esteem by praising their efforts and achievements, and providing support when they face challenges.

Mental Health Care: Pay attention to your children's mental health. Discuss emotions and seek professional help if necessary.

Celebrate Success: Celebrate your children's successes and achievements, no matter how small. This reinforces their sense of accomplishment and motivation.

Appreciation of the Little Things in Life: Focus on everyday happiness.

In the pursuit of prosperity in life, we often tend to focus on ambitious goals and major achievements. However, it is equally important to find joy and gratitude in the little things of everyday life. Appreciating the little things can enrich our lives and significantly contribute to a sense of well-being in all key areas of life. In "The Path to Prosperity," we explore why this approach is essential and how we can cultivate appreciation for the little things to increase our daily happiness.

The Importance of Appreciating the Little Things:

Improves Perspective: By focusing on the small positive things, we can change our perspective and find joy even in challenging times.

Reduces Stress: Gratitude and appreciation can help reduce stress by focusing on what is going well rather than worrying about what is lacking.

Promotes Connection: Appreciating the little things can strengthen relationships by making us more aware of the gestures of love and support from others.

Improves Mental Health: Practicing gratitude and appreciation has been linked to better mental health and greater life satisfaction.

How to Cultivate Appreciation for the Little Things:

Meditation and Mindfulness: Meditation and mindfulness are effective tools for training the mind to appreciate the present moment.

Gratitude Journaling: Keep a gratitude journal where you write down small things you're grateful for each day.

Practice Mindful Awareness: Take time to consciously observe your daily activities, savoring the details and paying attention to your senses.

Share Your Feelings: Express your appreciation to the people around you. Sharing your feelings of gratitude can often strengthen relationships.

Perform Acts of Kindness: Performing small acts of kindness towards others can generate a sense of satisfaction and joy.

Enjoy Nature: Connect with nature and appreciate its beauty. Going for a walk outdoors can renew your appreciation for the world around you.

Celebrate Everyday Moments: Celebrate everyday milestones, such as a delicious meal, a meaningful conversation, or a moment of quiet.

Unplug from Technology: Sometimes, unplugging from screens and technological distractions can help you better appreciate the real world.

Practice Family Gratitude: Foster gratitude in your family by sharing moments where each member expresses something they're grateful for.

Volunteering and Service: Serving others can generate a deep sense of gratitude and appreciation for what you have.

Learn from Experiences: Even challenges can provide valuable lessons. Reflect on what you've learned from difficulties.

Be Present: Instead of worrying about the past or the future, be mindful and grateful for the present moment.

Promote Empathy: Practice empathy by trying to understand others' experiences and perspectives.

Appreciate Art and Culture: Enjoy music, art, literature, and other forms of artistic expression that can inspire gratitude and appreciation.

Be Self-Compassionate: Treat yourself with kindness and self-compassion, acknowledging your achievements and efforts, no matter how small.

Celebration of Family Success: How to celebrate achievements and strengthen family bonds.

Celebrating success as a family is a powerful tool for strengthening family bonds and fostering an atmosphere of mutual support. In "The Path to Prosperity," we recognize the importance of acknowledging and celebrating achievements, big or small, as integral parts of prosperity in all key areas of life. Below, we explore why celebrating family success is essential and how you can incorporate this practice into your daily life.

The Importance of Celebrating Family Success:

Bond Strengthening: Celebrating success brings the family together by creating shared memories and fostering a sense of belonging and mutual support.

Boosting Self-Esteem: Celebrating personal and family achievements boosts the self-esteem of all family members, especially children.

Continuous Motivation: Recognition and celebration of success motivate everyone to strive for their goals and continue working together as a team.

Promotion of Gratitude: Celebrating success fosters gratitude by reminding the family of the blessings and opportunities they have.

How to Celebrate Family Success:

Sincere Recognition: The first step in celebrating family success is sincere recognition of achievements. Ensure that everyone feels valued and appreciated for their efforts.

Share Stories: Encourage family members to share their personal successes and achievements. Listen to their stories and celebrate their victories with them.

Celebration Rituals: Create family celebration rituals or traditions, such as a special dinner, a fun outing, or a family game night.

Awards and Recognition: Acknowledge achievements with symbolic awards and recognition, such as certificates, medals, or family trophies.

Achievement Album: Keep a family achievement album where you can record and remember successes over time.

Photos and Videos: Document celebratory moments with photos and videos that you can watch together in the future.

Congratulations Letters: Write congratulatory letters to family members when they achieve something significant. These letters can become emotional treasures.

Celebration of Goals Achieved: Celebrate reached goals enthusiastically, whether it's a new job, a promotion, an academic achievement, or any other significant milestone.

Birthday and Anniversary Celebrations: Take advantage of special occasions, such as birthdays and anniversaries, to celebrate personal and family successes.

Group Appreciation: Organize group appreciation sessions where each family member expresses gratitude to others for their support and contributions.

Group Volunteering: Work together as a family on volunteering projects to help others and celebrate the collective success of making a difference in the community.

Celebration of Effort: Don't just celebrate final achievements; also celebrate efforts and improvements along the way to success.

Set Family Goals: Define family goals and celebrate when they are achieved. This may include financial, health, or family relationship goals.

Teaching Values: Use the celebration of success as an opportunity to teach family values such as perseverance and collaboration.

Success Dinner: Organize a special success dinner where all family members share their achievements and goals.

Don't miss out!

Visit the website below and you can sign up to receive emails whenever Arthur Anderson publishes a new book. There's no charge and no obligation.

https://books2read.com/r/B-A-VJPZ-WSMZC

BOOKS 2 READ

Connecting independent readers to independent writers.

Also by Arthur Anderson

Las Mejores 20 Ideas para Ganar Dinero en Internet
Travesía Cósmica: Explorando los Límites del Universo"
El Misterio de El Risco Tenebroso: Secretos, Sacrificio y Redención
"The Mystery of the Dark Cliff: Secrets, Sacrifice, and Redemption"
Cosmic Journey: Exploring the Boundaries of the Universe
Las Mejores Ideas de Inversión con Poco Dinero y Buen Resultado
The Best 20 Ideas for Making Money Online
The Best Low-Capital Investment Ideas with Good Results
Henrik and the Ghost Island: The Legend of Zimbha Nau
Treasures and Betrayals: In Search of the Isle of Death
Henrik y la Isla Fantasma: La Leyenda de Zimbha Nau
Los Espíritus de Versaviz: Secretos de una Casa Antigua
Tesoros y Traiciones: En Busca de la Isla de la Muerte
The Spirits of Versaviz: Secrets of an Ancient House
The Three Kingdoms War: Battle for Seelanth
Asteroid X: Battle on the Alien Planet
Asteroid X: Batalla en el Planeta Alienígena
La Guerra de los Tres Reinos: Batalla por Seelanth
Pyros: El Juicio Final de la Humanidad
Pyros: the Final Judgment of Humanity
On the Trail of the Killer: Secrets Aboard
Tras las Huellas del Asesino: Secretos Abordo
La Lucha por Ucronix: la Última Frontera
The Struggle for Ucronix: The Final Frontier
20 hábitos Sencillos Para ser Buen Ciclista Amateur

www.ingramcontent.com/pod-product-compliance
Lightning Source LLC
Chambersburg PA
CBHW061635130726
47996CB00003B/1303